SONGS FROM
FROZEN, TANGLED AND ENCHANTED

To access audio visit:
www.halleonard.com/mylibrary

Enter Code
4073-1331-9505-8364

Disney characters and artwork © Disney Enterprises, Inc.

ISBN 978-1-4803-8720-1

WALT DISNEY MUSIC COMPANY
WONDERLAND MUSIC COMPANY, INC.

DISTRIBUTED BY

7777 W. BLUEMOUND RD. P.O. BOX 13819 MILWAUKEE, WI 53213

In Australia Contact:
Hal Leonard Australia Pty. Ltd.
4 Lentara Court
Cheltenham, Victoria, 3192 Australia
Email: ausadmin@halleonard.com.au

Visit Hal Leonard Online at
www.halleonard.com

DO YOU WANT TO BUILD A SNOWMAN?

from Disney's Animated Feature FROZEN

Music and Lyrics by KRISTEN ANDERSON-LOPEZ
and ROBERT LOPEZ

4

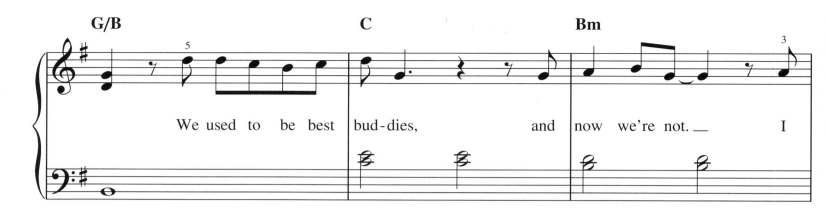

G/B   **C**   **Bm**

We used to be best bud-dies, and now we're not. __ I

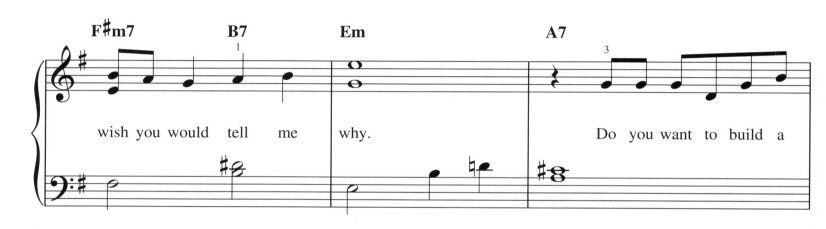

F♯m7   **B7**   **Em**   **A7**

wish you would tell me why. Do you want to build a

Am   **Cm6/E♭**

snow - man? It does-n't have to be a snow - man.

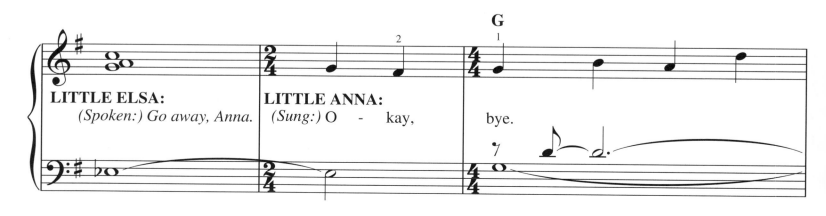

G

LITTLE ELSA:
(Spoken:) Go away, Anna.

LITTLE ANNA:
(Sung:) O - kay, bye.

YOUNG ANNA:

Do you want to build a snow - man?

(knocking)

mf

Or ride our bike a-round the halls? I think some com-pan - y is

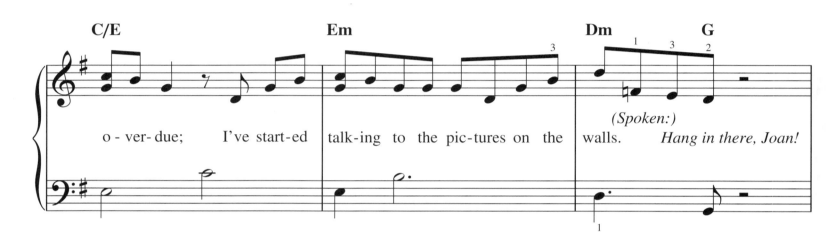

o - ver-due; I've start-ed talk-ing to the pic-tures on the walls. *(Spoken:) Hang in there, Joan!*

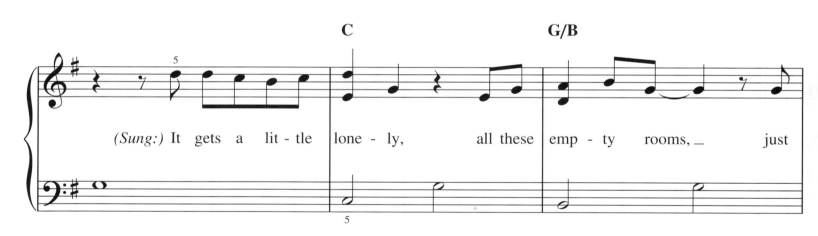

(Sung:) It gets a lit - tle lone - ly, all these emp - ty rooms, __ just

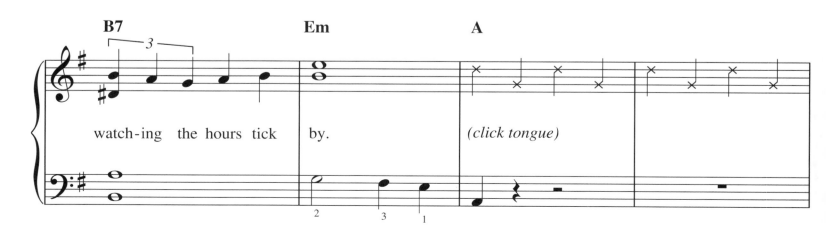

watch-ing the hours tick by. *(click tongue)*

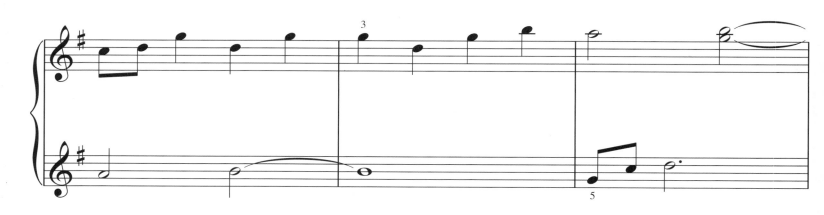

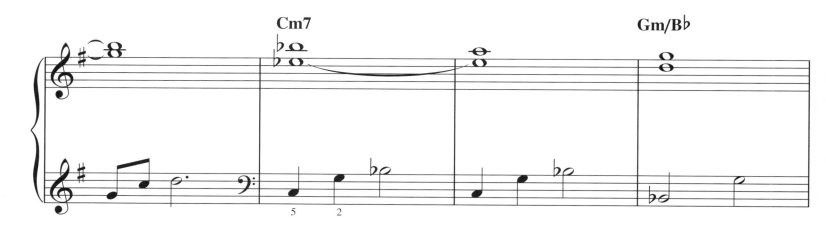

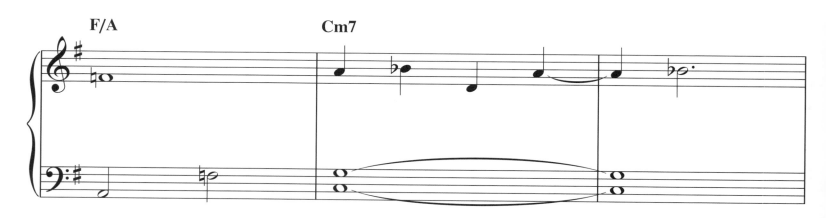

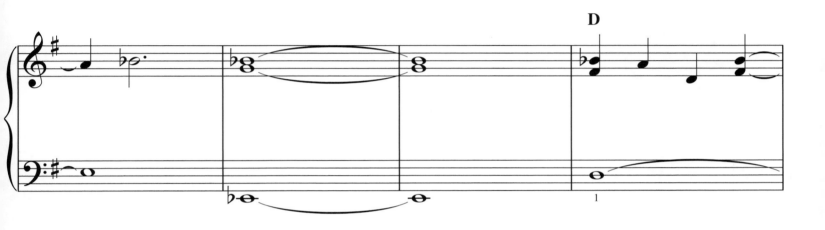

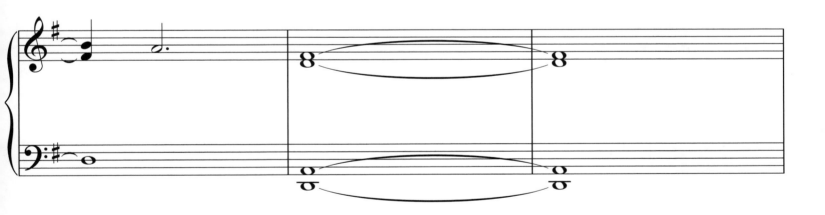

(knocking) *(Spoken:)* Elsa? *(Sung:)* Please,   I   know you're   in   there.

Peo-ple are ask-ing where you've been. They say, "Have cour-age," and I'm

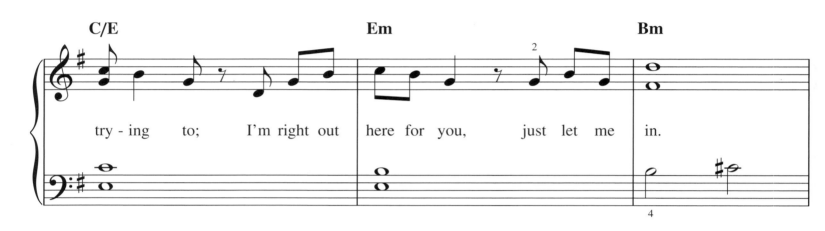

try - ing to; I'm right out here for you, just let me in.

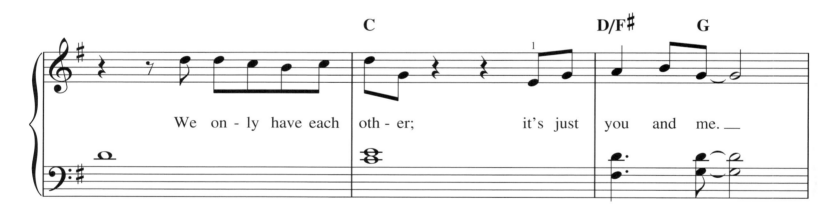

We on - ly have each oth - er; it's just you and me.

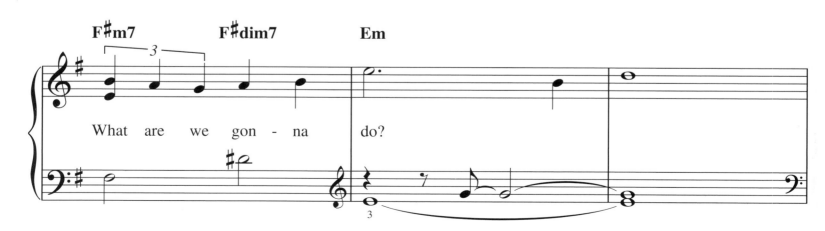

What are we gon - na do?

Do you want to build a snow - man?

FOR THE FIRST TIME IN FOREVER

from Disney's Animated Feature FROZEN

Music and Lyrics by KRISTEN ANDERSON-LOPEZ
and ROBERT LOPEZ

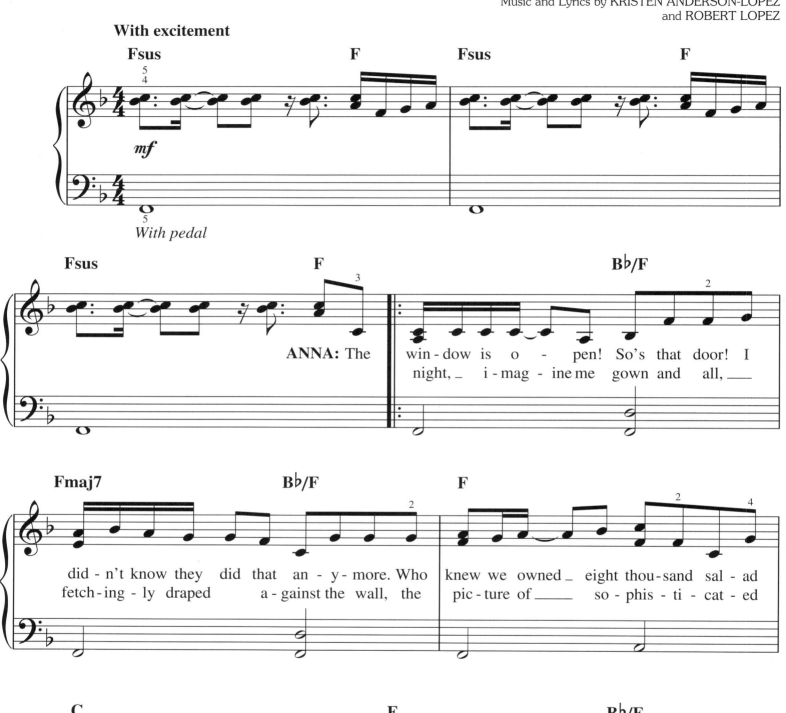

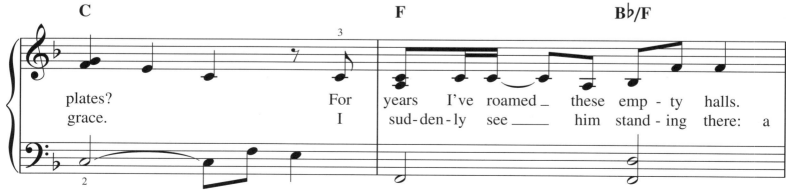

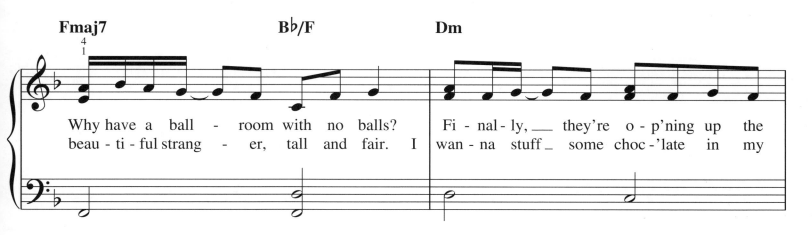

Why have a ball - room with no balls?
beau - ti - ful strang - er, tall and fair. I

Fi - nal - ly, ___ they're o - p'ning up the
wan - na stuff ___ some choc - 'late in my

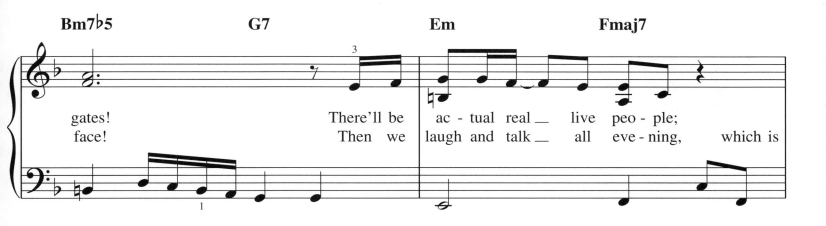

gates!
face!

There'll be
Then we

ac - tual real ___ live peo - ple;
laugh and talk ___ all eve - ning, which is

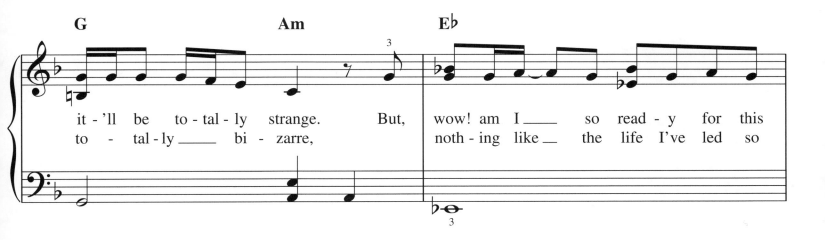

it - 'll be to - tal - ly strange. But,
to - tal - ly ___ bi - zarre,

wow! am I ___ so read - y for this
noth - ing like ___ the life I've led so

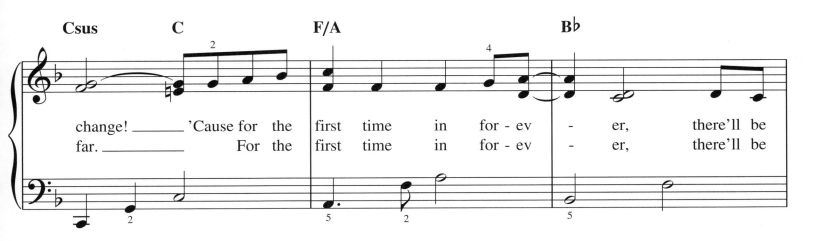

change! ___ 'Cause for the first time in for - ev - er, there'll be
far. ___ For the first time in for - ev - er, there'll be

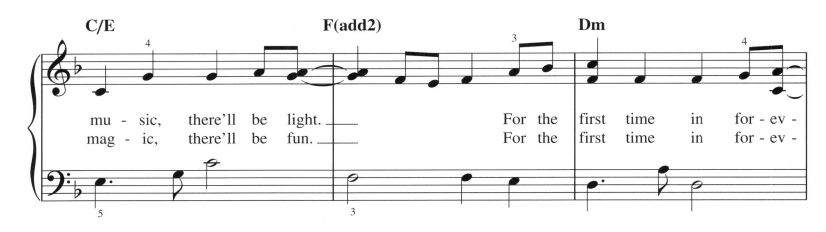

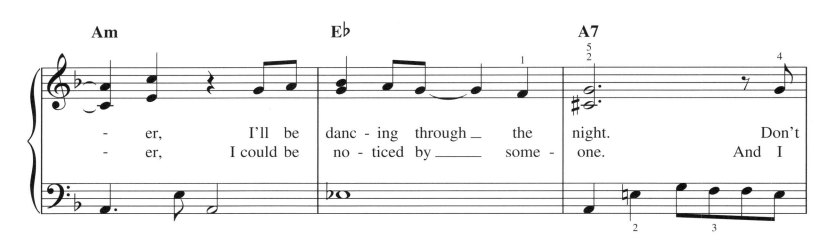

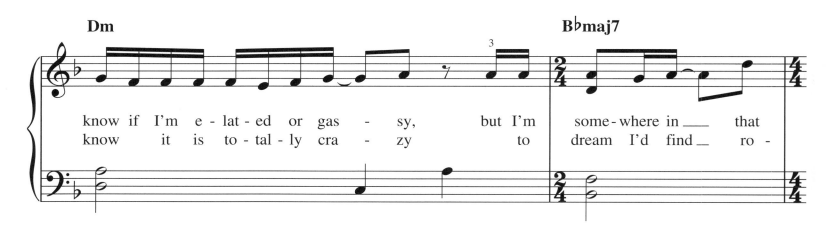

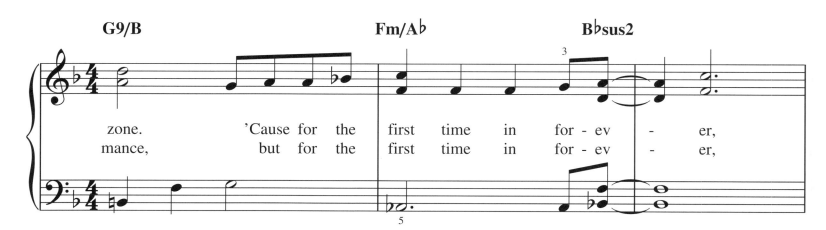

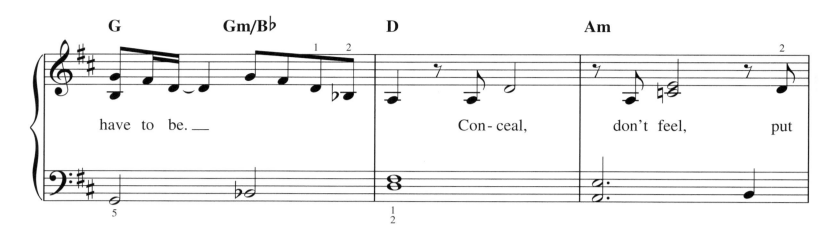

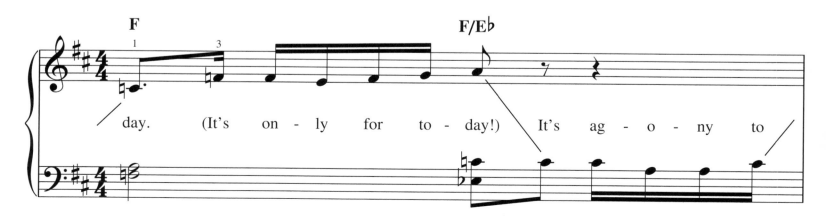

wait! (It's ag - o - ny to wait!) Tell the guards to o - pen up the

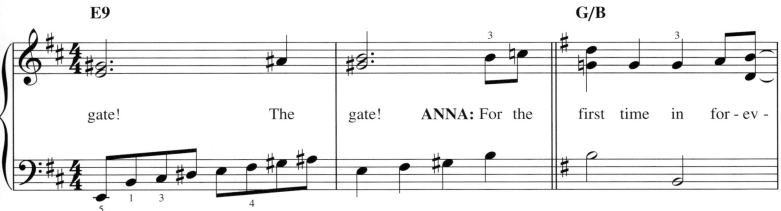

gate! The gate! **ANNA:** For the first time in for - ev -

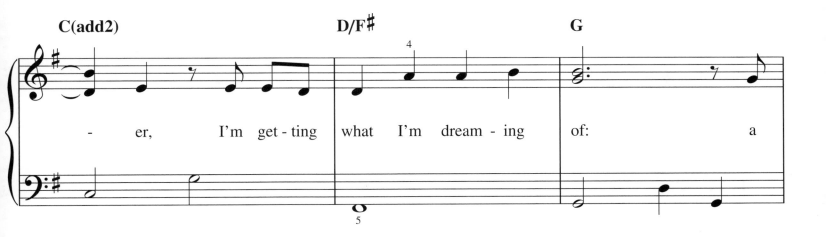

- er, I'm get - ting what I'm dream - ing of: a

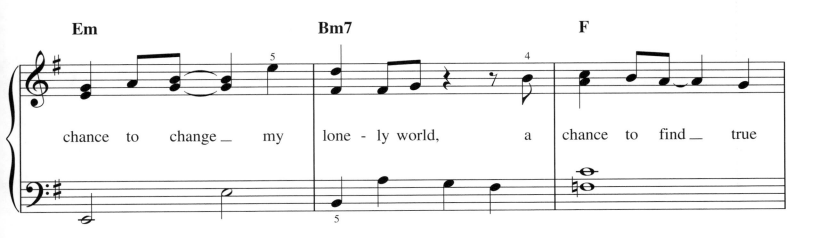

chance to change __ my lone - ly world, a chance to find __ true

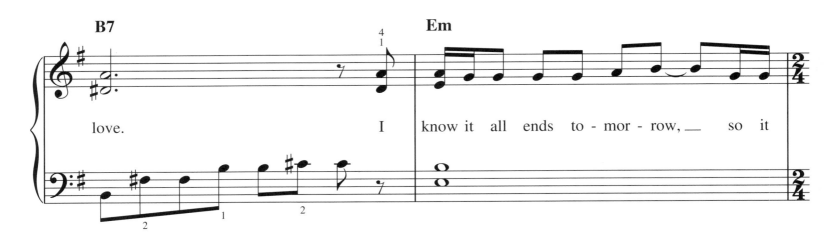

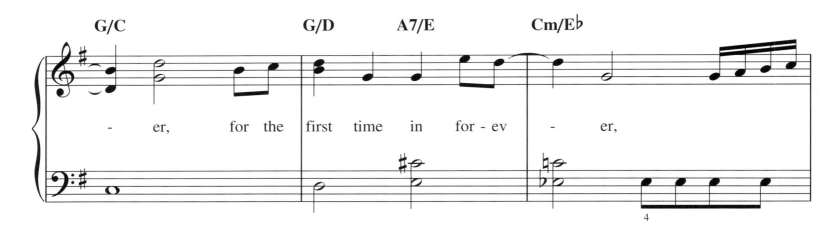

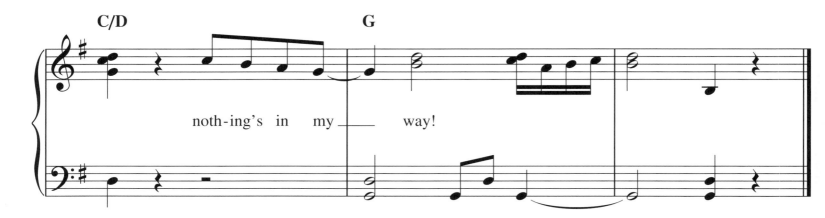

LET IT GO
from Disney's Animated Feature FROZEN

Music and Lyrics by KRISTEN ANDERSON-LOPEZ
and ROBERT LOPEZ

Half-time feel, mysterious

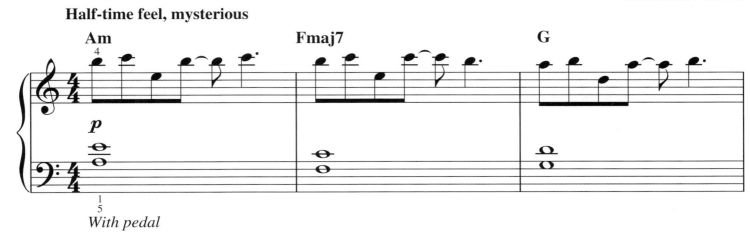

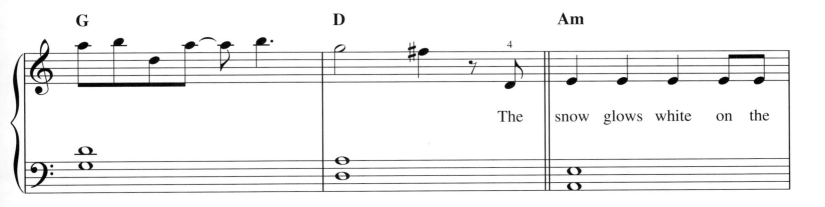

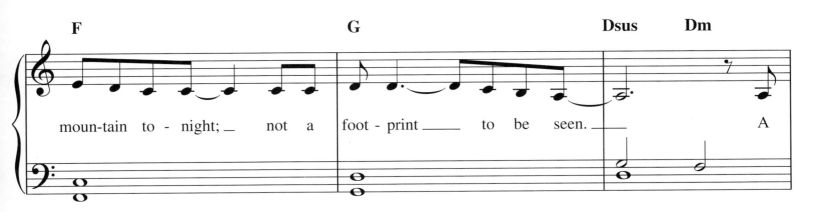

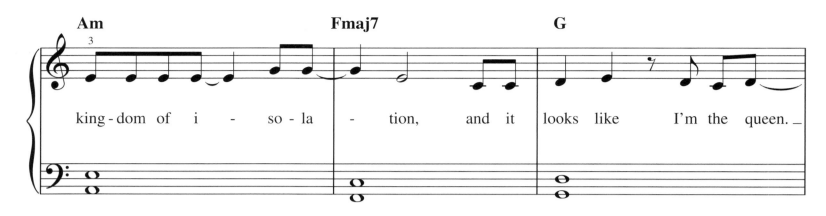

king-dom of i - so-la - tion, and it looks like I'm the queen.

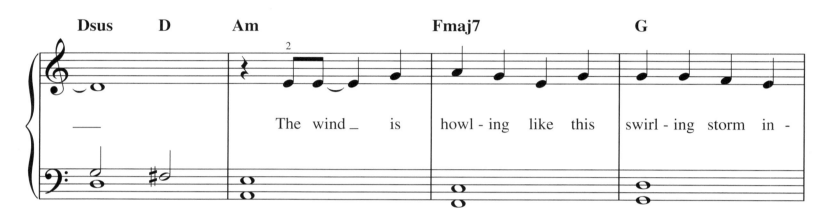

The wind is howl-ing like this swirl-ing storm in-

side. Could-n't keep it in, heav-en knows I

tried. Don't let them in, don't let them

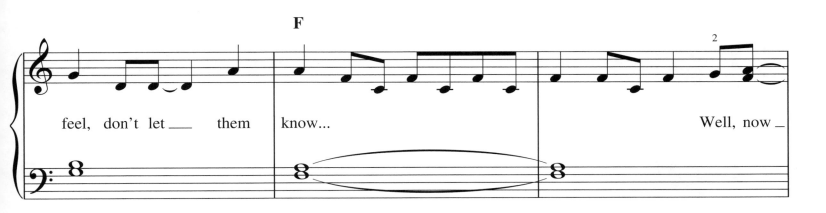

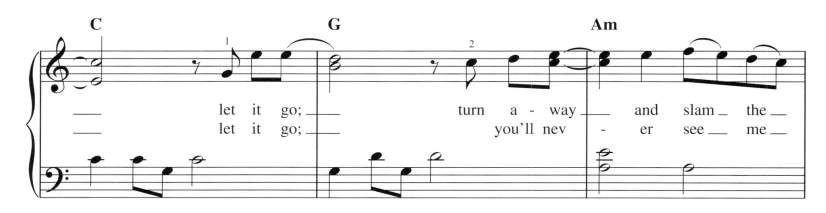

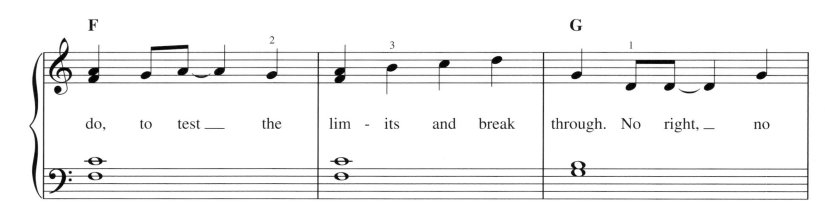

do, to test ___ the lim - its and break through. No right, ___ no

wrong, no rules for me, ___ I'm free!

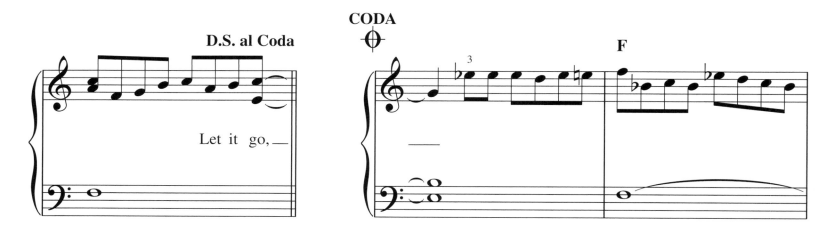

D.S. al Coda

Let it go, ___

CODA

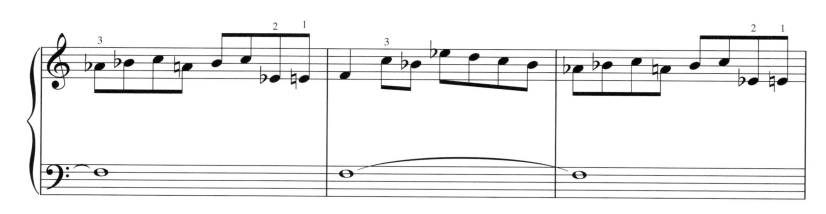

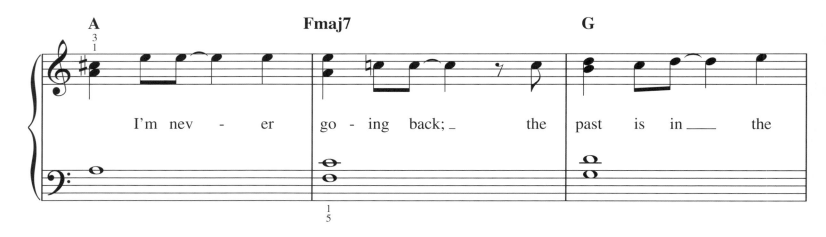

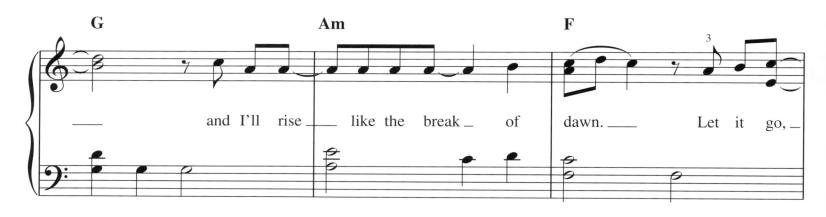

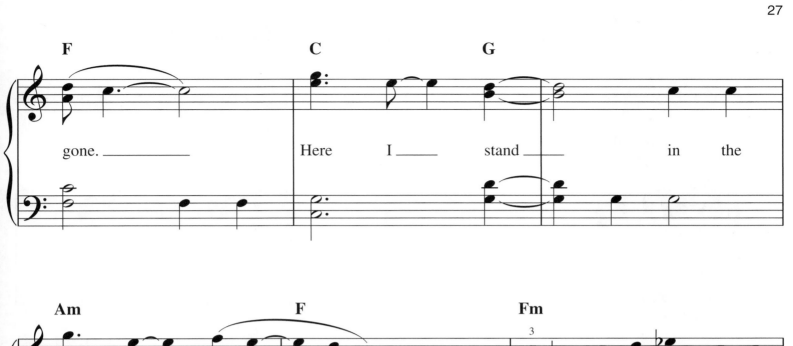

gone. _____ Here I ___ stand ___ in the

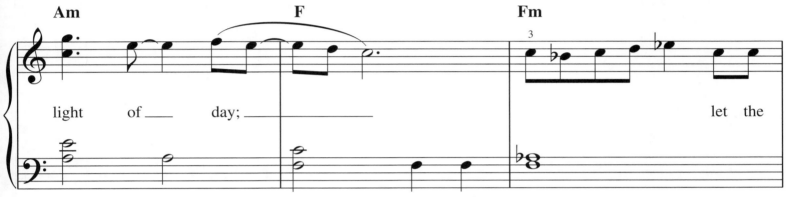

light of ___ day; _____ let the

storm rage _ on. _____ The

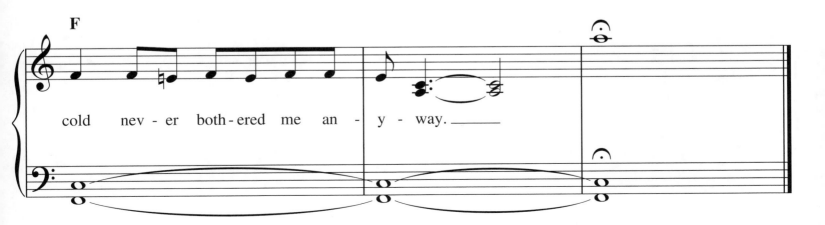

cold nev - er both-ered me an - y - way. _____

LOVE IS AN OPEN DOOR

from Disney's Animated Feature FROZEN

Music and Lyrics by KRISTEN ANDERSON-LOPEZ
and ROBERT LOPEZ

32

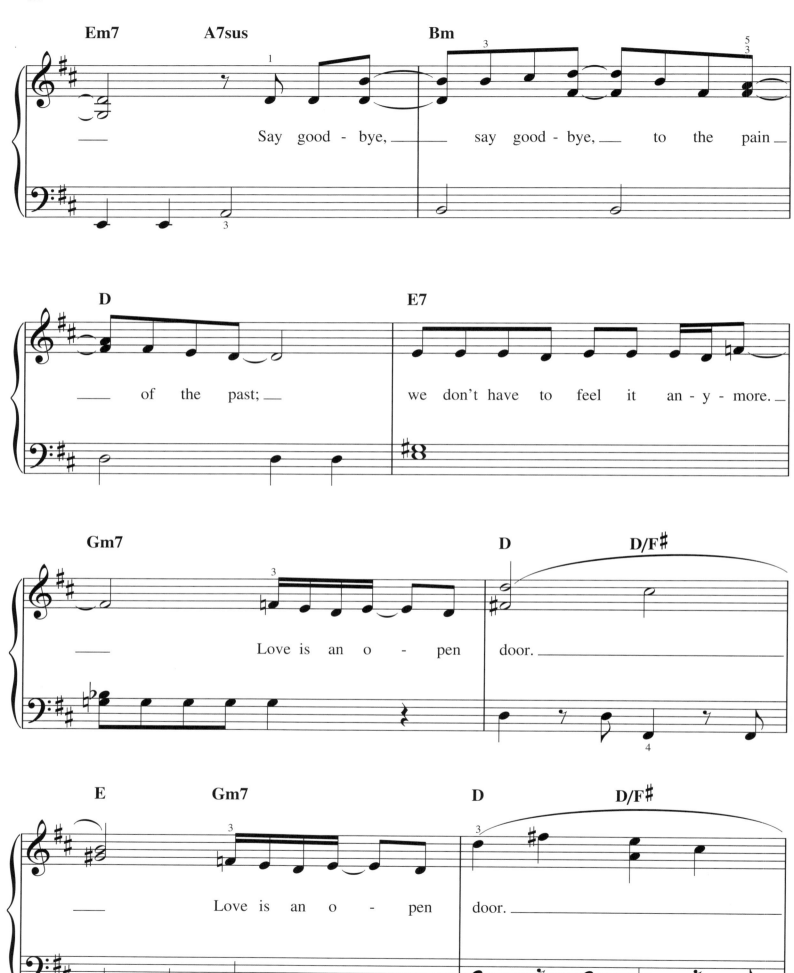

I SEE THE LIGHT
from Walt Disney Pictures' TANGLED

Music by ALAN MENKEN
Lyrics by DAVID SLATER

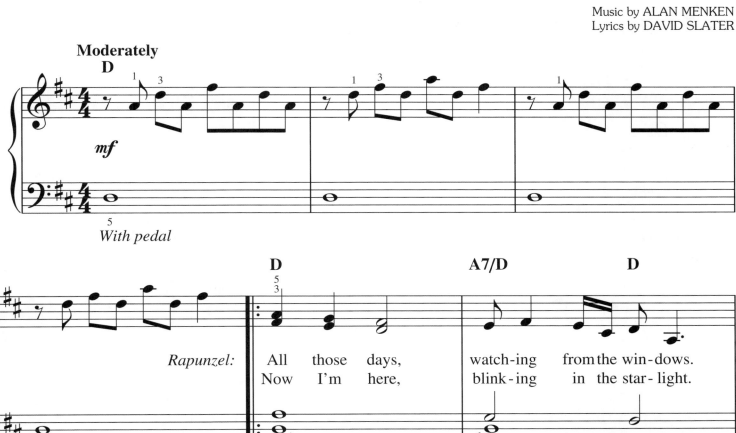

Rapunzel: All those days, watch-ing from the win-dows.
Now I'm here, blink-ing in the star-light.

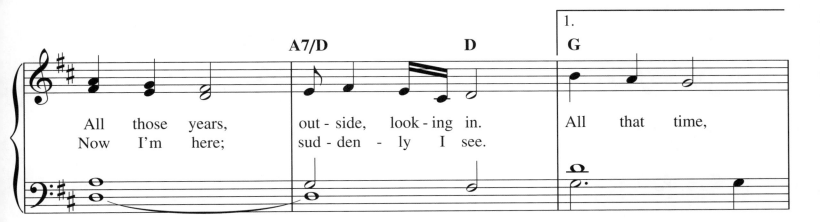

All those years, out - side, look - ing in.
Now I'm here; sud - den - ly I see.

All that time,

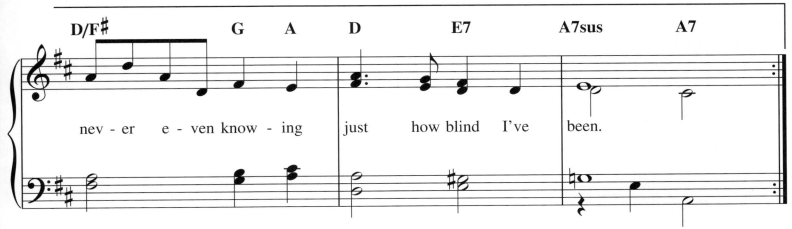

nev - er e - ven know - ing just how blind I've been.

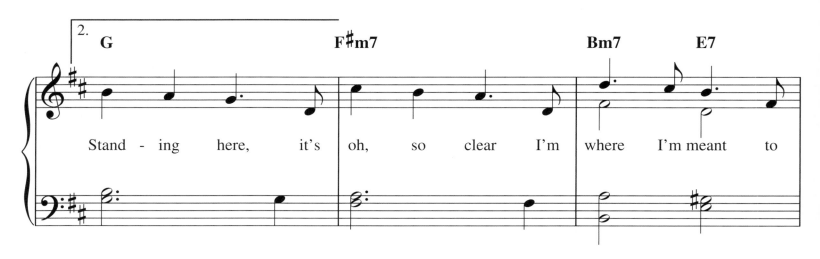

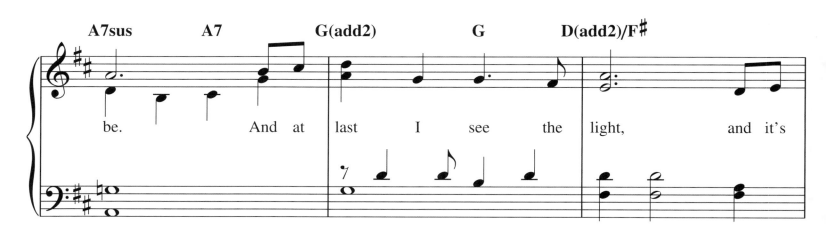

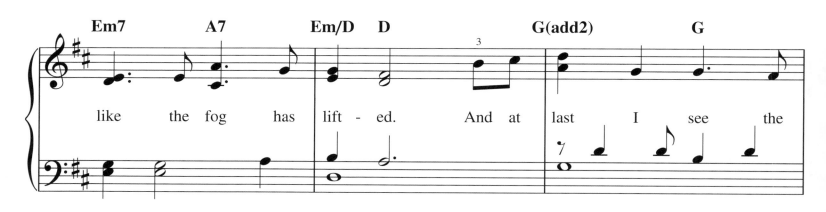

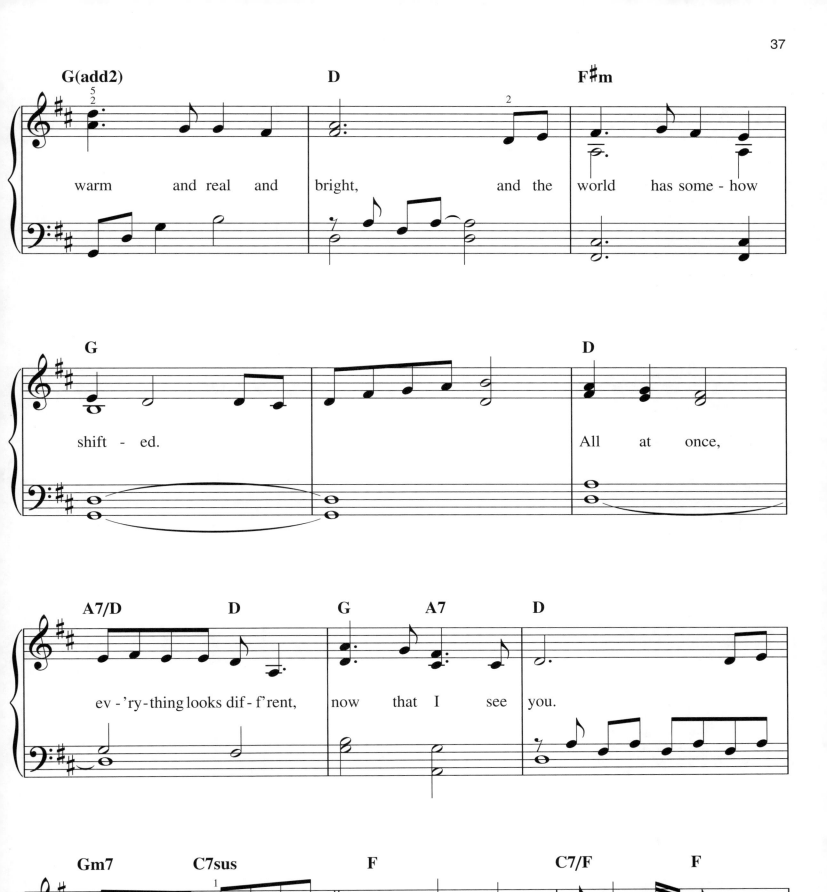

All those years liv-ing in a blur. All that time,

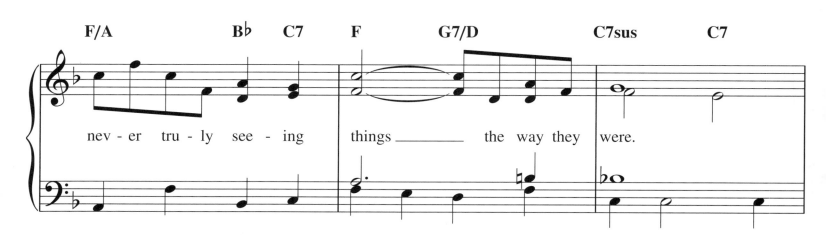

nev-er tru-ly see-ing things _____ the way they were.

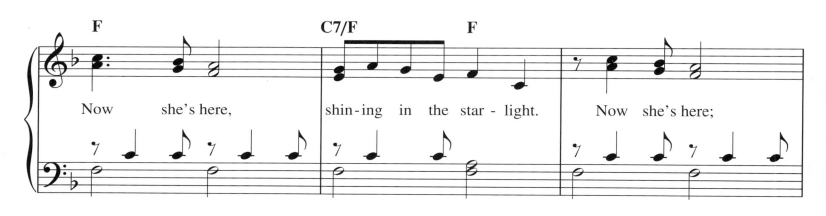

Now she's here, shin-ing in the star-light. Now she's here;

sud-den-ly I know: if she's here, it's crys-tal clear I'm

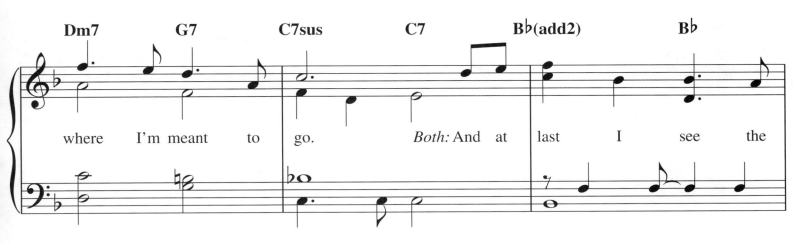

where I'm meant to go. *Both:* And at last I see the

light, *Flynn:* and it's like the fog has lift - ed. *Both:* And at

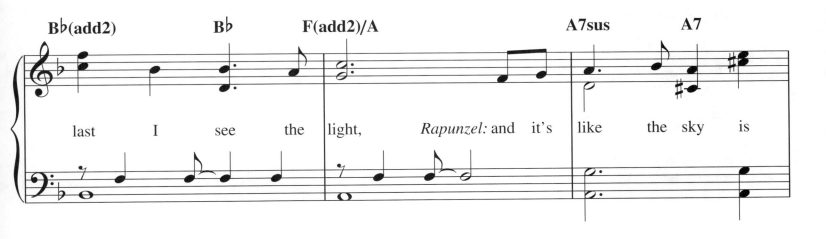

last I see the light, *Rapunzel:* and it's like the sky is

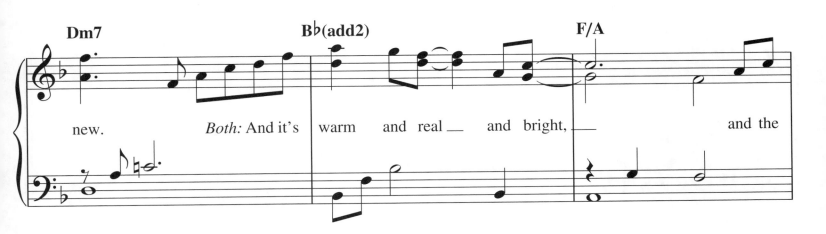

new. *Both:* And it's warm and real ___ and bright, ___ and the

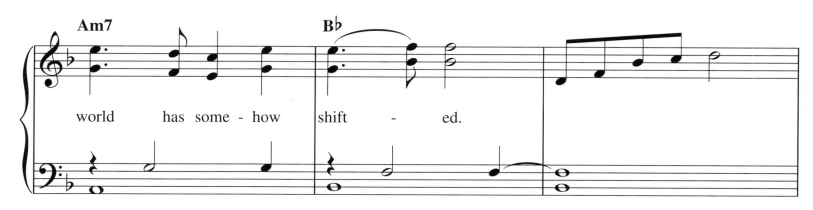

world has some - how shift - ed.

All at once, ev - 'ry - thing is dif - f'rent, now that I see

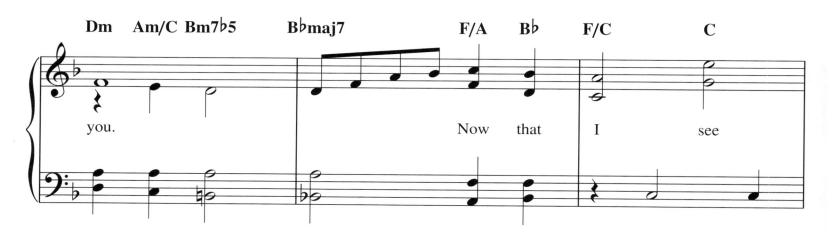

you. Now that I see

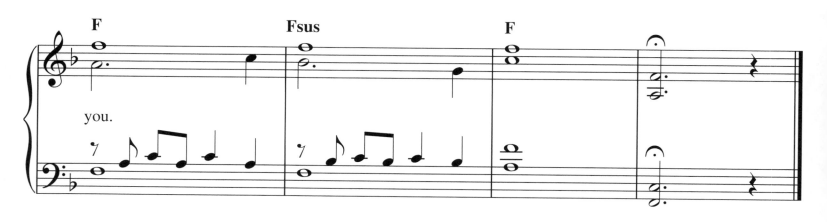

you.

I'VE GOT A DREAM
from Walt Disney Pictures' TANGLED

Music by ALAN MENKEN
Lyrics by GLENN SLATER

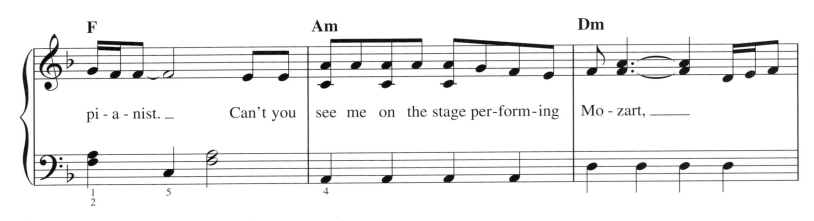

pi - a - nist. _____ Can't you see me on the stage per-form-ing Mo - zart, _____

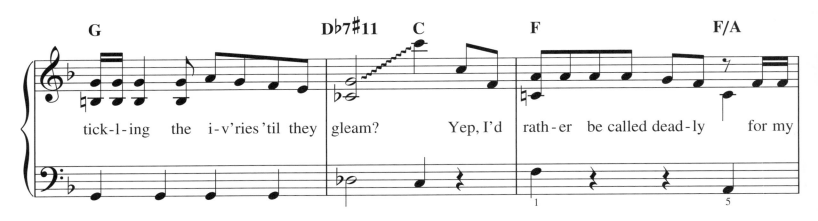

tick-l-ing the i-v'ries 'til they gleam? Yep, I'd rath-er be called dead-ly for my

kill - er show - tune med - ley. Thank you! 'Cause

way down deep in-side, I've got a dream. _____ He's got a dream, _____ he's got a

Thug Chorus:

dream.   See, I   ain't as cruel and   vi - cious as   I   seem.   Though I

Hook Hand Thug:

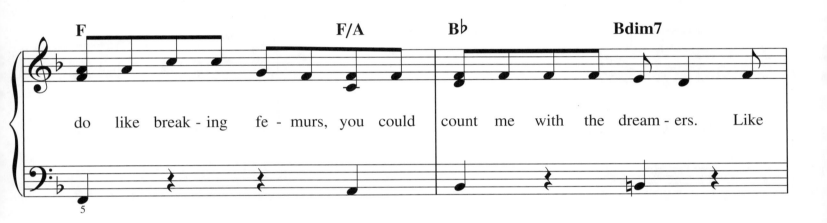

do   like   break - ing   fe - murs, you could   count   me   with   the   dream - ers.   Like

ev - 'ry - bod - y   else, I've   got   a   dream.   Na   na   na   na   na   na   na   na   na

Thug Chorus:

na   na   na   na   na.   I've got   scars and lumps and bruis - es, ___   plus

Big Nose Thug:

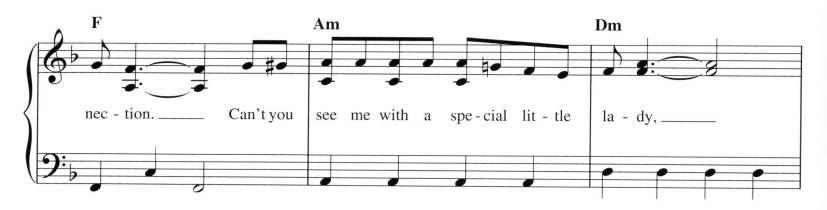

lov-er,   not a fight-er,   'cause way down deep in-side, I've got a   dream.   I've got a

dream, _____ I've got a   dream,   and I   know one day ro-mance will reign su -

preme!   Though my face leaves peo-ple scream-ing, there's a   child be-hind it dream-ing.   Like

ev-'ry-bod-y else, I've got a   dream.   *Thug Chorus:* Tor would like to quit and be   a

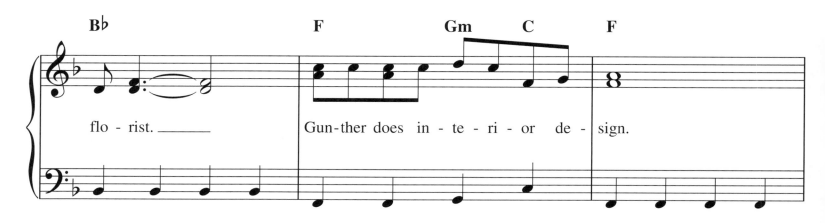

flo - rist. _____ Gun-ther does in - te - ri - or de - sign.

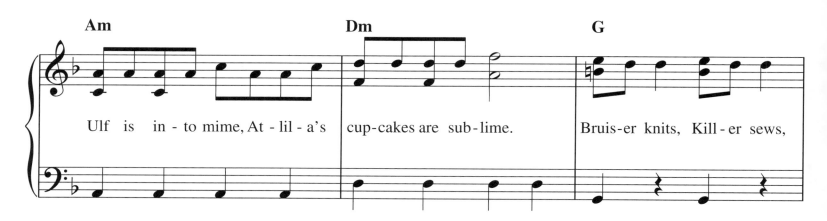

Ulf is in - to mime, At - lil - a's cup-cakes are sub-lime. Bruis-er knits, Kill - er sews,

Hook Hand Thug:

Fang does lit - tle pup-pet shows, and Vla - di - mir col-lects cer - am - ic u - ni - corns.

rit.

Flynn: I have dreams like you, no, real- ly! Just much less touch-y feel- y. They

a tempo

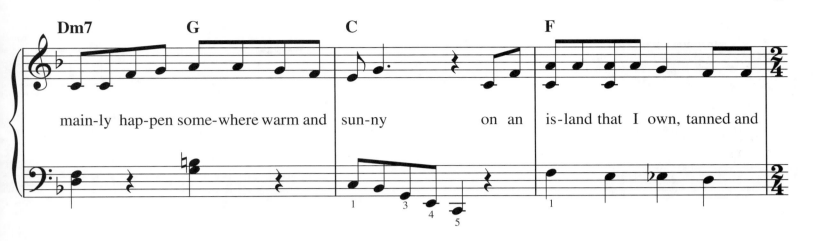

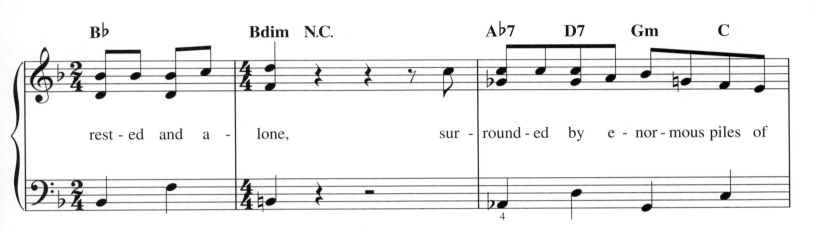

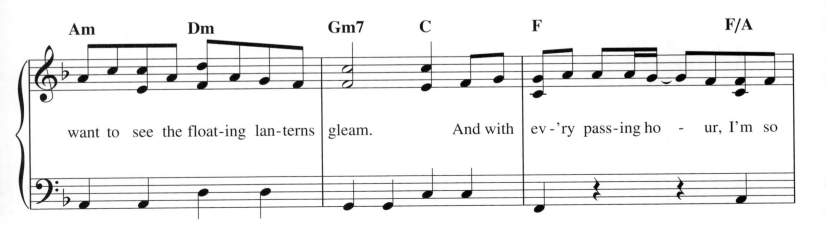

glad I left my tow- er. Like all you love-ly folks, I've got a dream. _____ *Thug Chorus:* She's got a

dream, _____ we've got a dream. So our dif-f'renc-es ain't real - ly that ex -

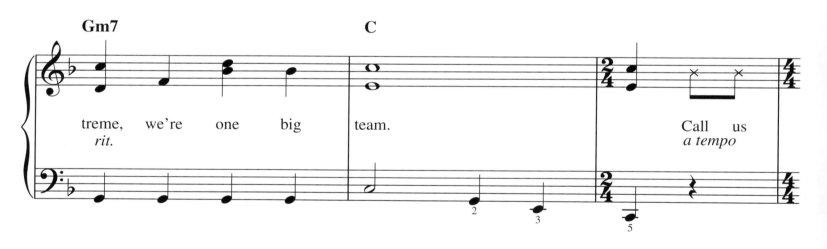

treme, we're one big team. Call us
rit. *a tempo*

Hook Hand Thug: *Big Nose Thug:* *Thug Chorus:*
bru - tal, sick, sa - dis - tic, and gro - tes - quely op - ti - mis - tic. 'Cause

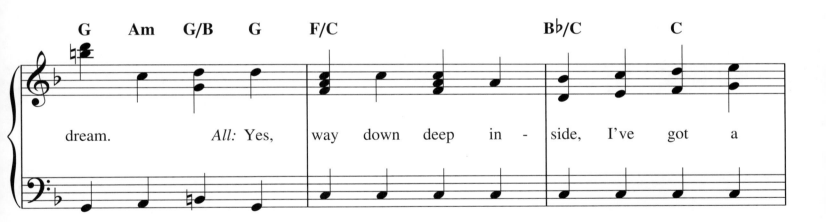

WHEN WILL MY LIFE BEGIN

from Walt Disney Pictures' TANGLED

Music by ALAN MENKEN
Lyrics by GLENN SLATER

Moderately fast Rock

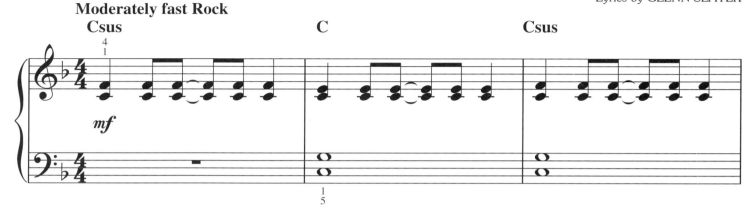

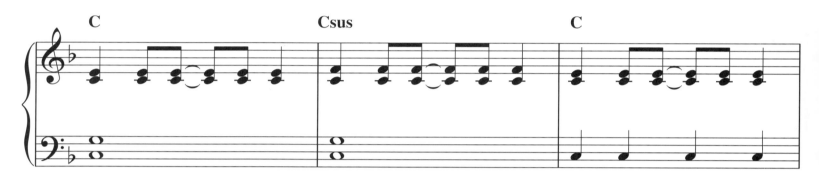

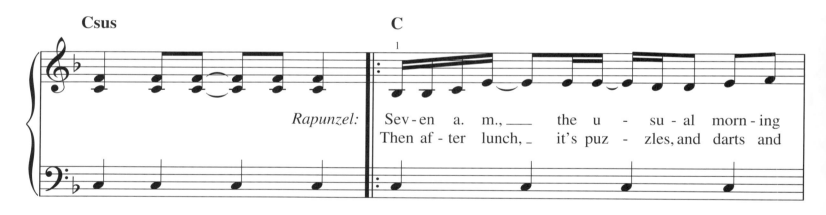

Rapunzel: Sev-en a. m., ___ the u - su-al morn-ing
Then af-ter lunch, _ it's puz - zles, and darts and

line - up. ___
bak - ing... ___

Start on the chores, _ and sweep _ 'til the floor's all
pa-per mâ-ché, ___ a bit ___ of bal - let and

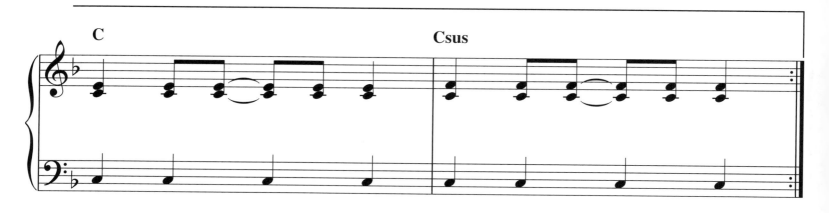

just like they do on ___ my birth - day ___ each

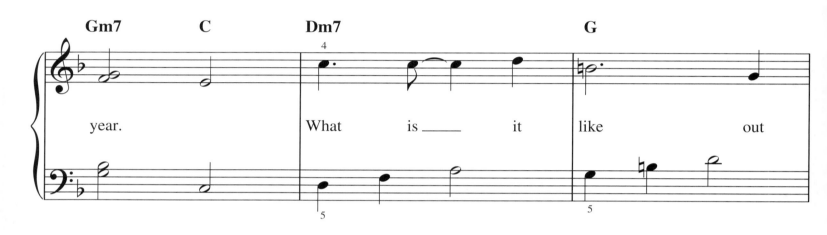

year. What is ___ it like out

there where they glow? Now that I'm

old - er, ___ Moth - er might just ___ let me go...

HAPPY WORKING SONG
from Walt Disney Pictures' ENCHANTED

Music by ALAN MENKEN
Lyrics by STEPHEN SCHWARTZ

Perky and light

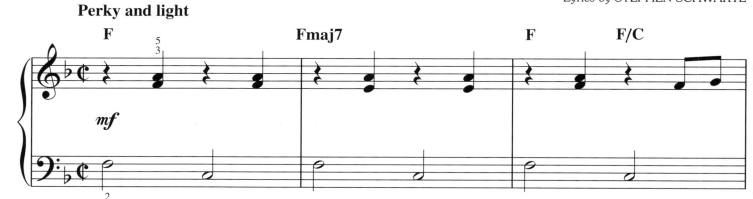

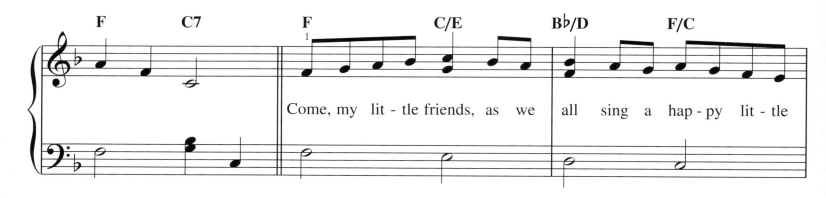

Come, my lit - tle friends, as we all sing a hap - py lit - tle

work - ing song, mer - ry lit - tle voic - es clear and strong.

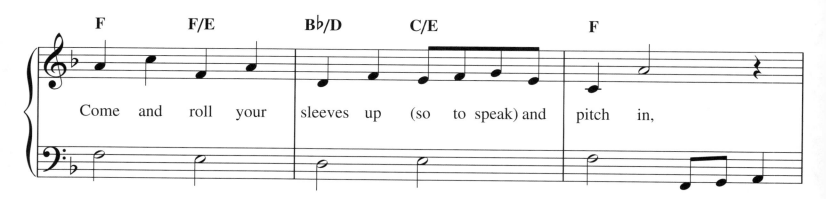

Come and roll your sleeves up (so to speak) and pitch in,

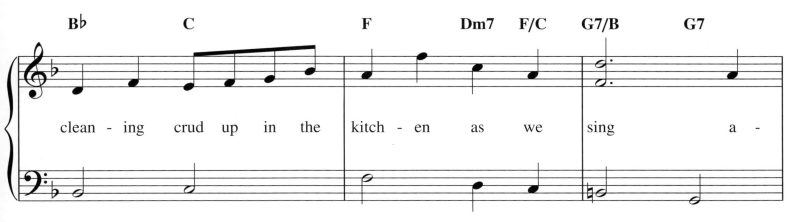

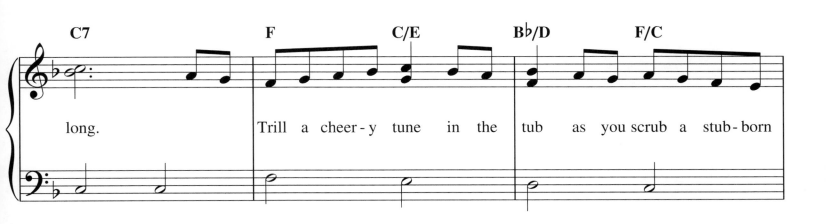

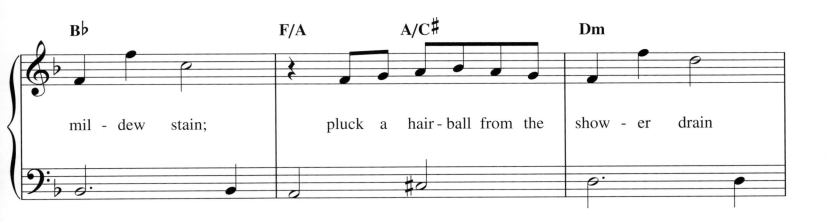

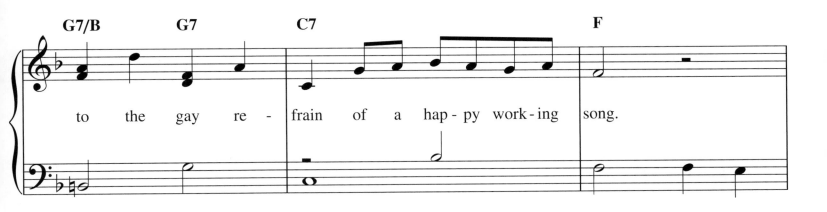

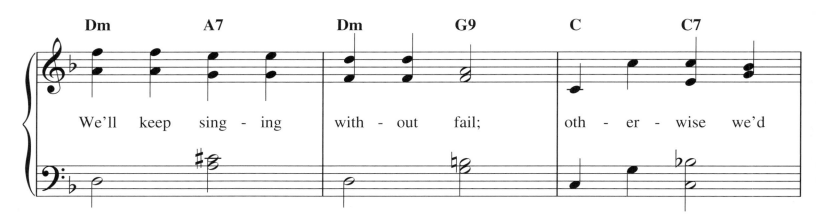

We'll keep sing - ing with - out fail; oth - er - wise we'd

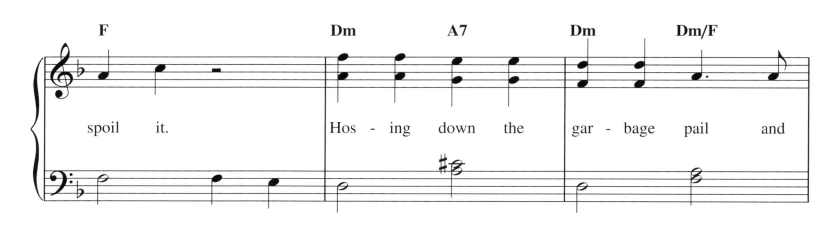

spoil it. Hos - ing down the gar - bage pail and

scrub - bing up the toi - let! Oh, how we all en - joy let - ting

loose with a lit - tle "la da dum dum dum" while we're emp - ty - ing the

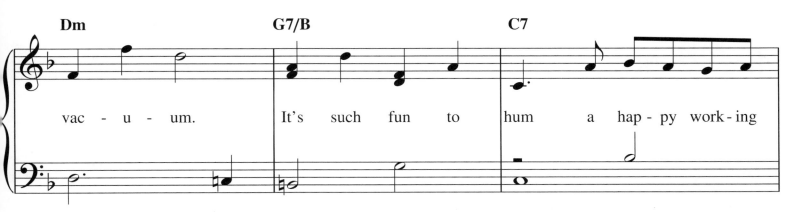

vac - u - um.   It's   such   fun   to   hum   a   hap - py   work - ing

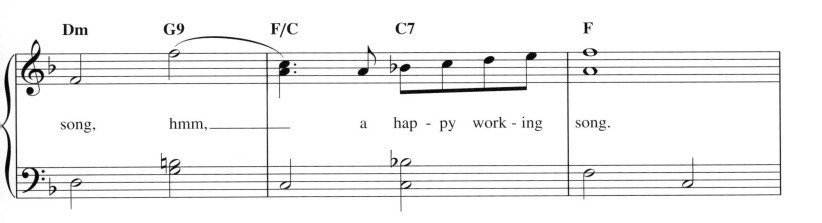

song,   hmm,____   a   hap - py   work - ing   song.

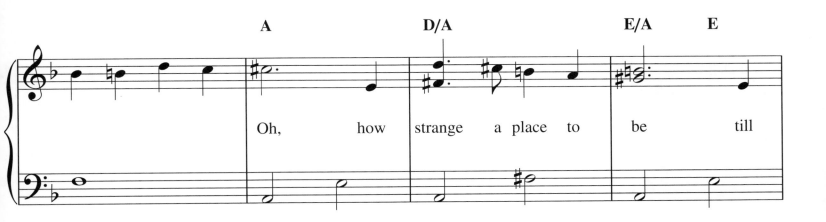

Oh,   how   strange   a   place   to   be   till

Ed - ward   comes   for   me!   My   heart   is

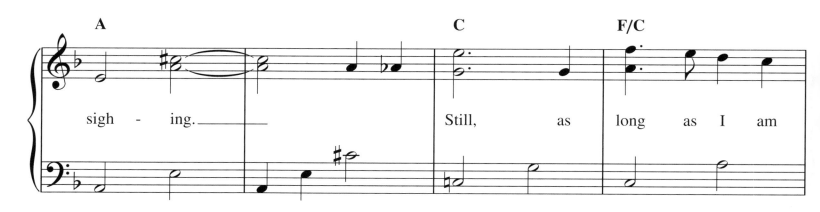

sigh - ing. _____ Still, as long as I am

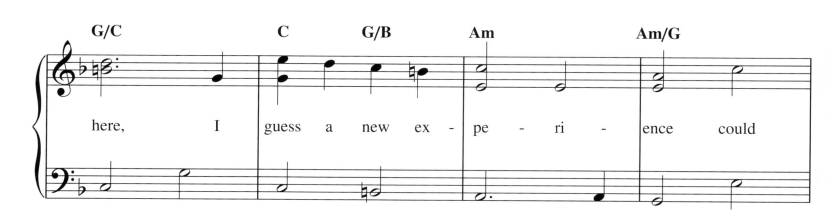

here, I guess a new ex - pe - ri - ence could

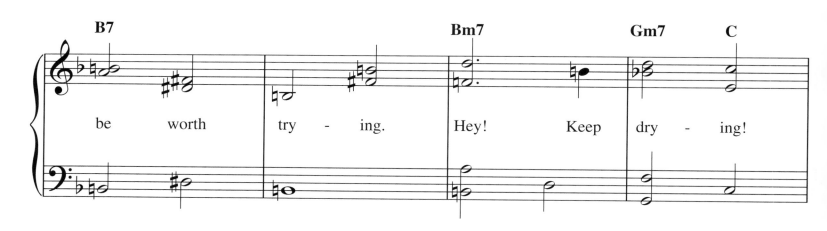

be worth try - ing. Hey! Keep dry - ing!

You can do a lot when you've got such a hap - py work-ing tune to hum

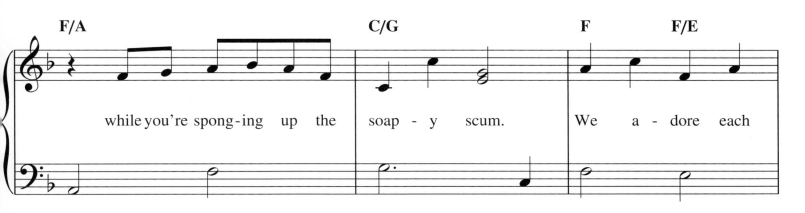

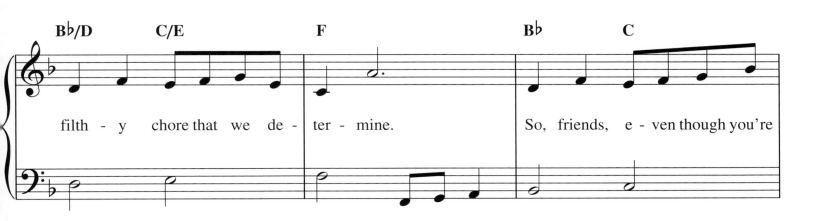

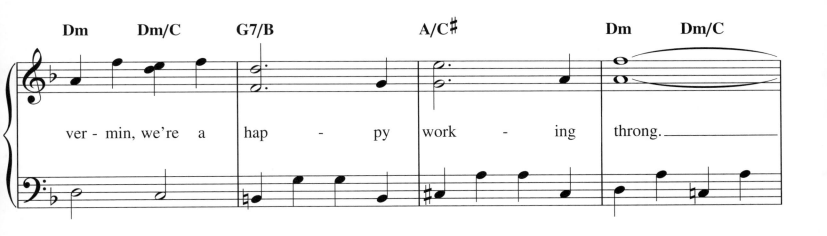

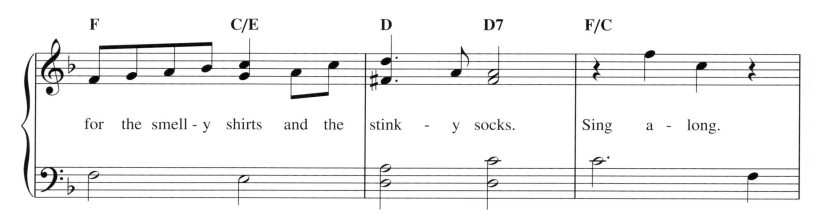

for the smell-y shirts and the stink - y socks. Sing a - long.

If you can-not sing, then hum a - long as we're fin-ish-ing our

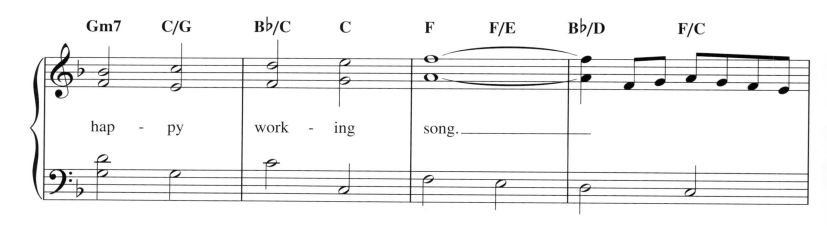

hap - py work - ing song.

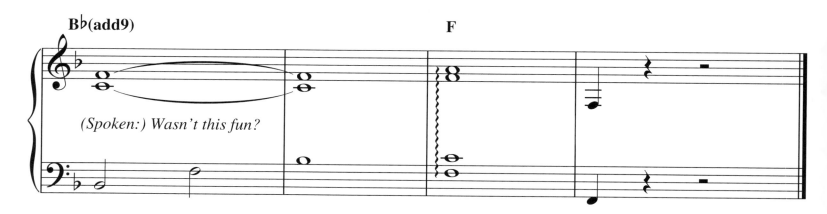

(Spoken:) Wasn't this fun?

THAT'S HOW YOU KNOW
from Walt Disney Pictures' ENCHANTED

Music by ALAN MENKEN
Lyrics by STEPHEN SCHWARTZ

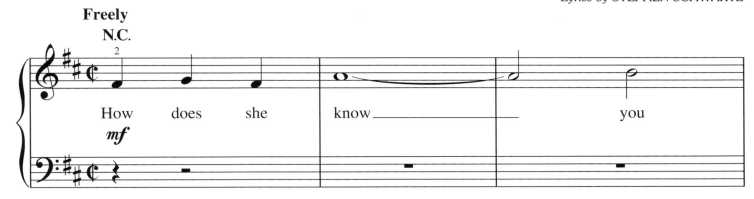

How does she know that you love her?

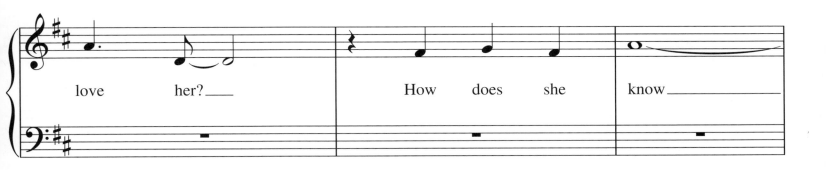

love her? How does she know

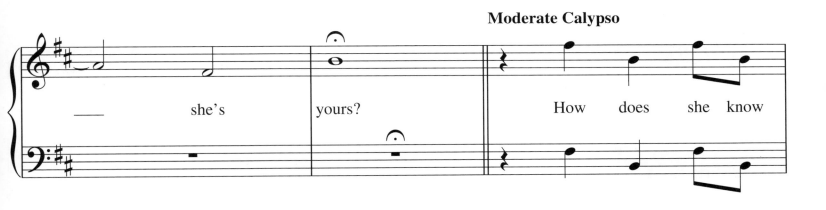

she's yours? **Moderate Calypso** How does she know

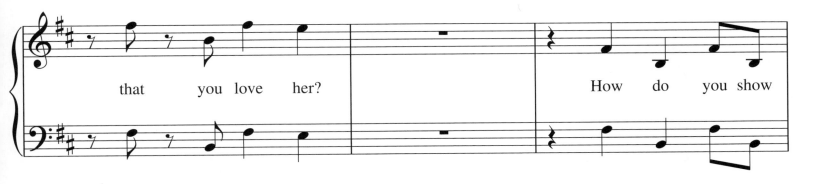

that you love her? How do you show

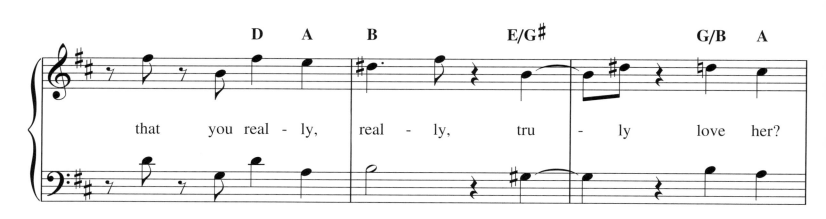

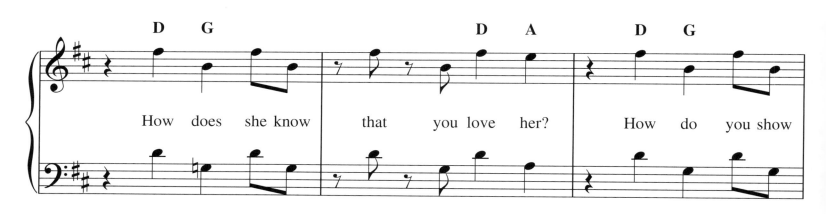

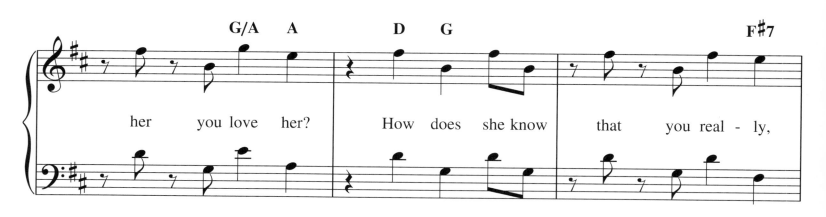

B · E · G A · %· D

real - ly, tru - ly love her? It's not e - nough to take
Ev - 'ry-bod-y wants to live

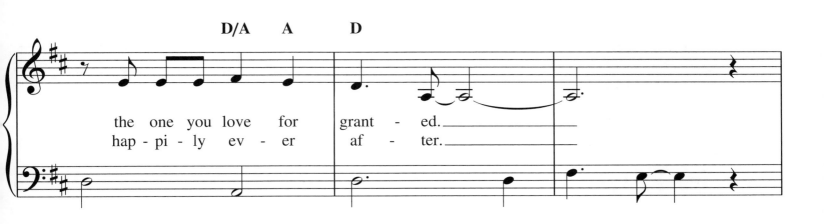

D/A · A · D

the one you love for grant - ed.____
hap - pi - ly ev - er af - ter.____

A F# · B

You must re - mind her, or____ she'll be in-clined to say:____
Ev - 'ry-bod - y wants to know____ their true____ love is true.____

E · G/A A7 · D · Em · G/A

____ "How do I know he
____ How do you know he

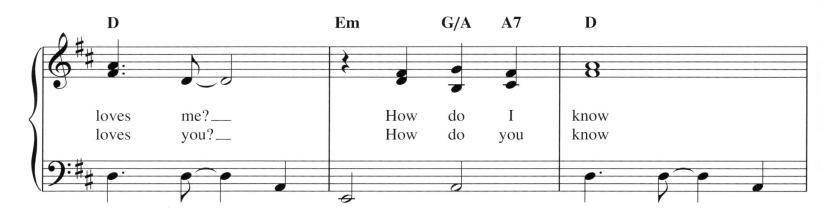

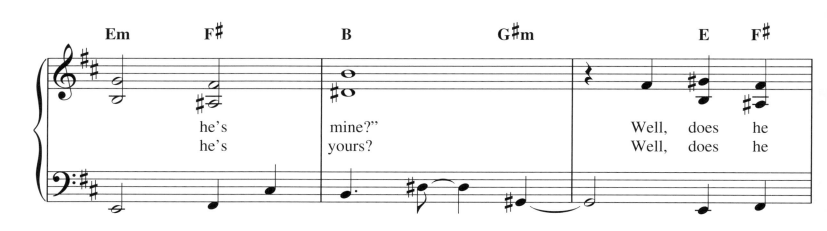

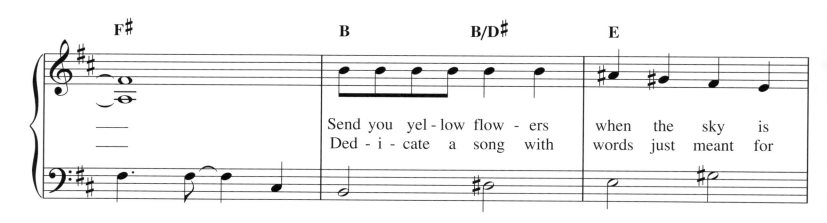

You've got to show her you need her; don't treat her like

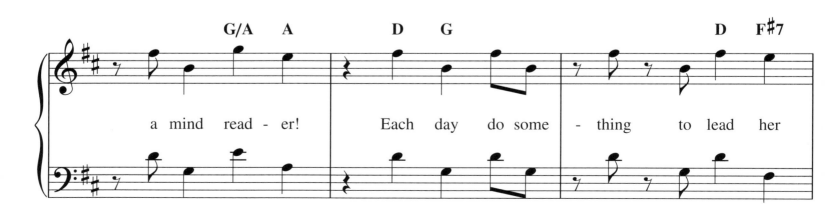

a mind read - er! Each day do some - thing to lead her

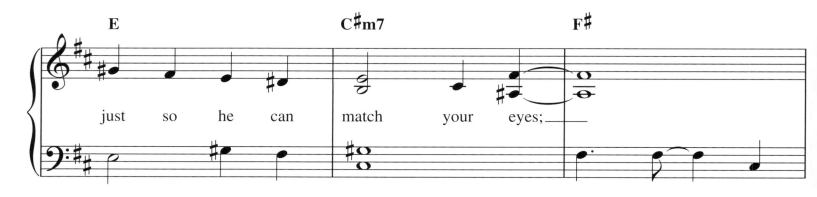

just so he can match your eyes;

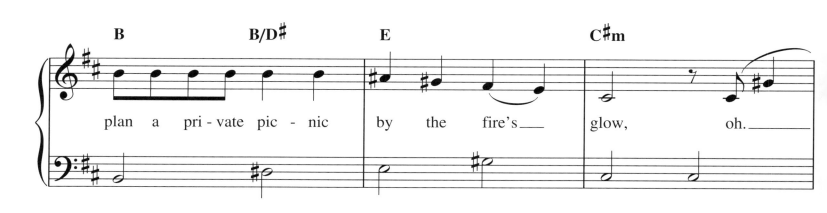

plan a pri - vate pic - nic by the fire's glow, oh.

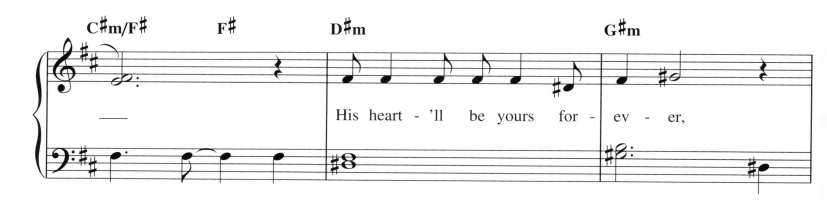

His heart - 'll be yours for - ev - er,

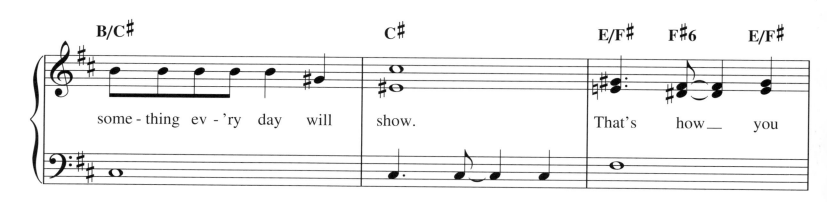

some - thing ev - 'ry day will show. That's how you

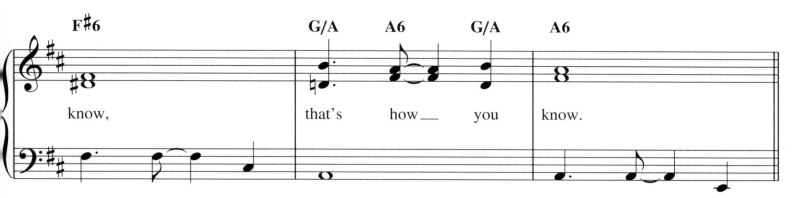

know,   that's how___ you know.

That's how___ you know,   that's how___ you

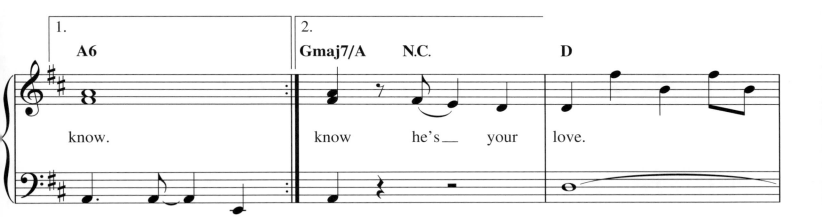

1.
know.   2. know he's___ your love.

That's how you show her you love her.

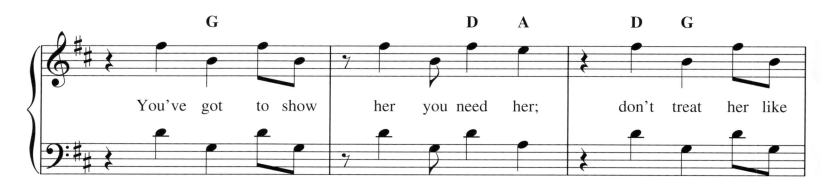

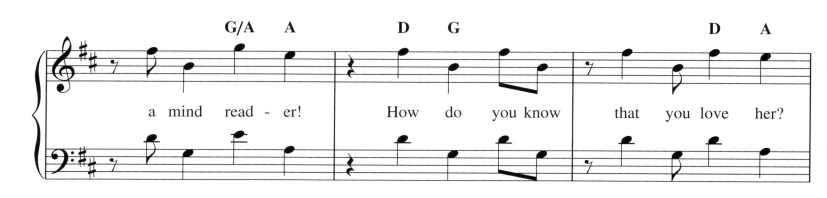

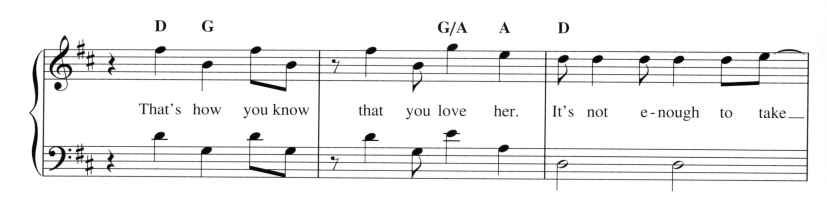

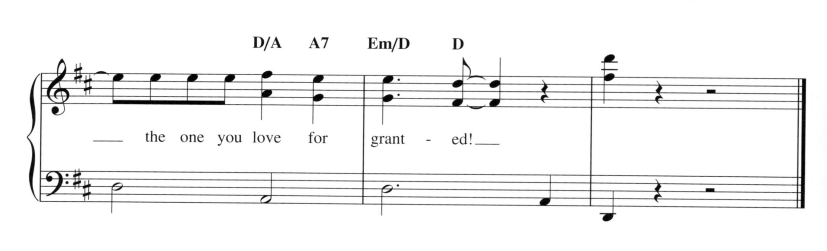

TRUE LOVE'S KISS
from Walt Disney Pictures' ENCHANTED

Music by ALAN MENKEN
Lyrics by STEPHEN SCHWARTZ

Easily, with freedom

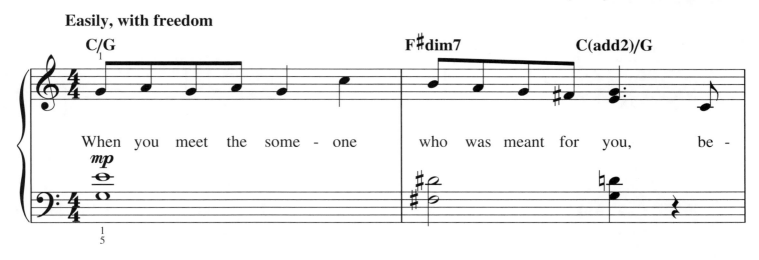

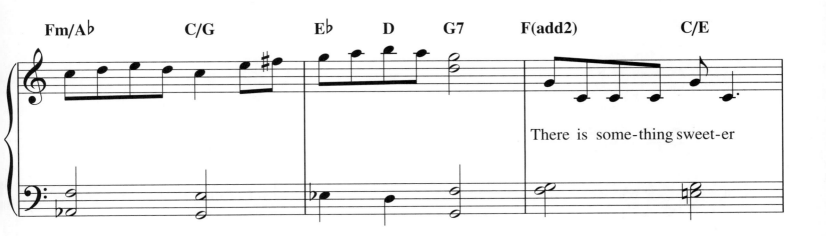

More flowing, still freely

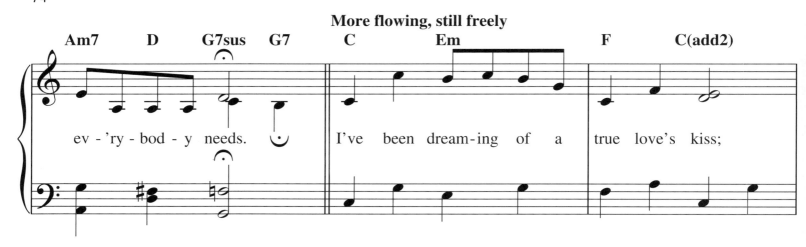

ev - 'ry - bod - y needs. I've been dream-ing of a true love's kiss;

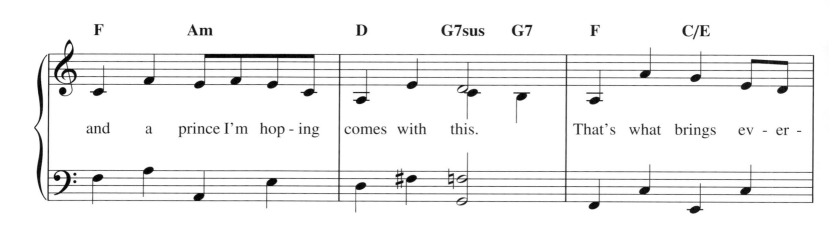

and a prince I'm hop - ing comes with this. That's what brings ev - er -

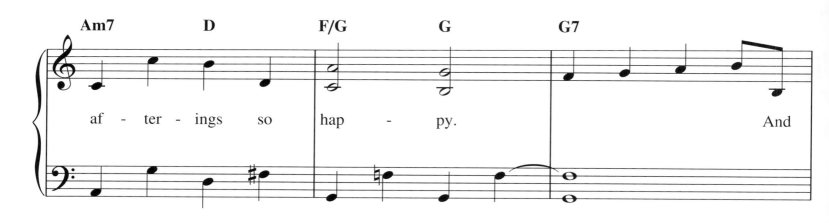

af - ter - ings so hap - py. And

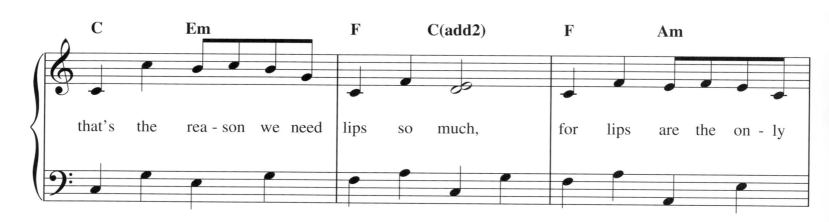

that's the rea - son we need lips so much, for lips are the on - ly

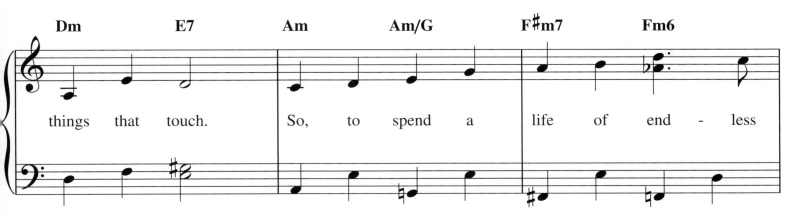

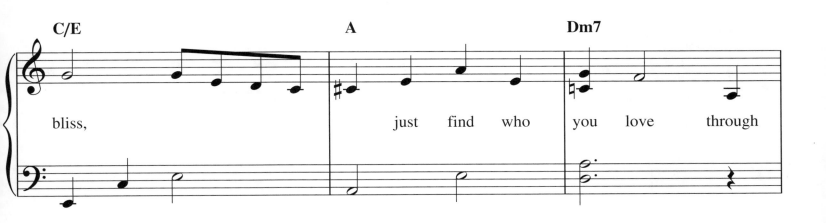

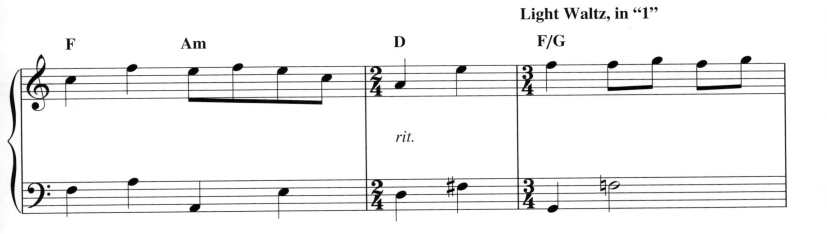

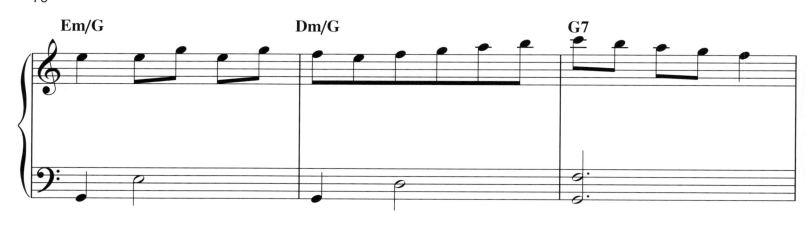

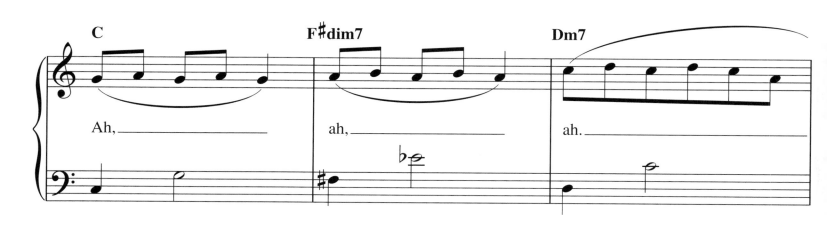

Ah,_____ ah,_____ ah._____

Ah,_____ ah,_____

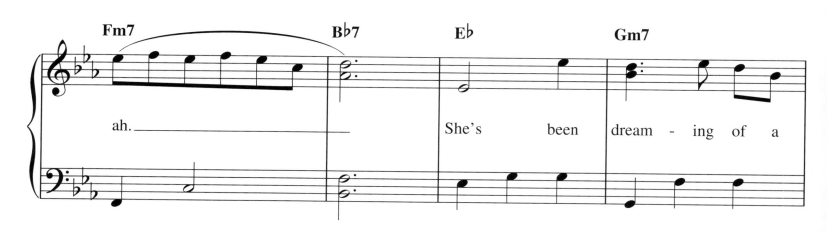

ah._____ She's been dream - ing of a

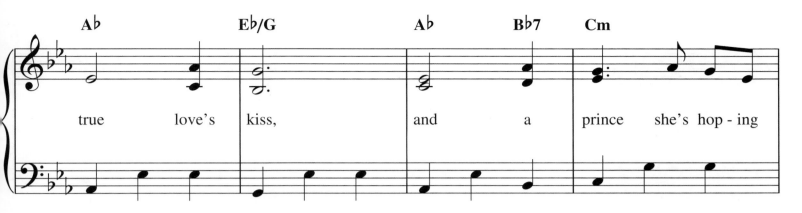

true love's kiss, and a prince she's hop - ing

comes with this. That's what brings ev - er -

af - ter - ings so hap - py.

And that's the rea - son we need

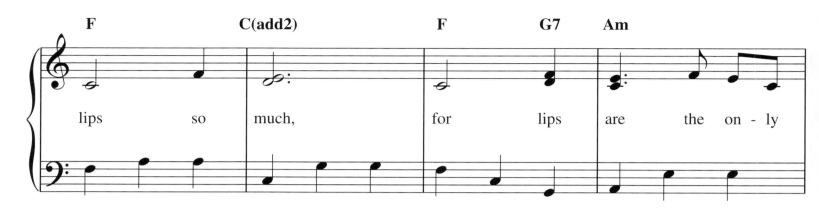

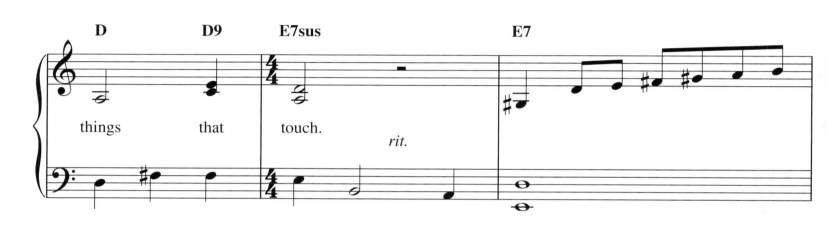

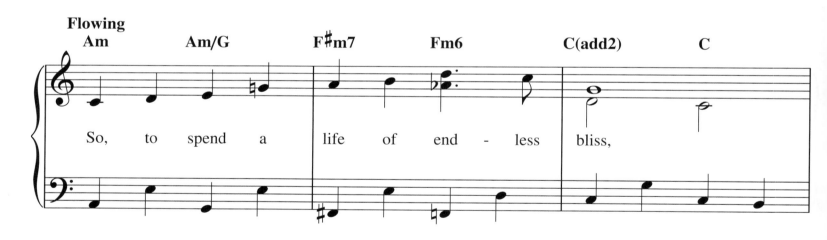